IN THE
NATIONAL INTEREST

General Sir John Monash once exhorted a graduating class to 'equip yourself for life, not solely for your own benefit but for the benefit of the whole community'. At the university established in his name, we repeat this statement to our own graduating classes, to acknowledge how important it is that common or public good flows from education.

Universities spread and build on the knowledge they acquire through scholarship in many ways, well beyond the transmission of this learning through education. It is a necessary part of a university's role to debate its findings, not only with other researchers and scholars, but also with the broader community in which it resides.

Publishing for the benefit of society is an important part of a university's commitment to free intellectual inquiry. A university provides civil space for such inquiry by its scholars, as well as for investigations by public intellectuals and expert practitioners.

This series, In the National Interest, embodies Monash University's mission to extend knowledge and encourage informed debate about matters of great significance to Australia's future.

Professor Susan Elliott AM
Interim President and Vice-Chancellor,
Monash University

PAUL FARRELL

GLADYS: A LEADER'S UNDOING

MONASH
UNIVERSITY
PUBLISHING

Gladys: A Leader's Undoing
© Copyright 2023 Paul Farrell
All rights reserved. Apart from any uses permitted by Australia's *Copyright Act 1968*, no part of this book may be reproduced by any process without prior written permission from the copyright owners. Inquiries should be directed to the publisher.

Monash University Publishing
Matheson Library Annexe
40 Exhibition Walk
Monash University
Clayton, Victoria 3800, Australia
https://publishing.monash.edu

Monash University Publishing brings to the world publications which advance the best traditions of humane and enlightened thought.

ISBN: 9781922633538 (paperback)
ISBN: 9781922633552 (ebook)

Series: In the National Interest
Editor: Greg Bain
Project manager & copyeditor: Paul Smitz
Designer: Peter Long
Typesetter: Cannon Typesetting
Proofreader: Gillian Armitage
Printed in Australia by Ligare Book Printers

A catalogue record for this book is available from the National Library of Australia.

GLADYS: A LEADER'S UNDOING

It was a grey day in Sydney on 12 October 2020 when Gladys Berejiklian stepped into a witness box, triggering a chain of events that would ultimately lead to her resignation. She had been called to give evidence at an anti-corruption inquiry held by the Independent Commission Against Corruption (ICAC) into Daryl Maguire. The former Wagga Wagga MP had allegedly turned his electoral office into a bazaar of side hustles that he attempted to benefit from, and he'd been accused of the brazen misuse of his political influence.

Just days earlier, Berejiklian had said she was 'pleased' to be giving evidence. She made it all sound very casual, like ICAC had invited her over for dinner. Indeed, the indications were that this was all just procedural. As the NSW premier of the day, Berejiklian oversaw the conduct of her ministers and parliamentary secretaries. It made sense she would be called on to discuss potential breaches of the ministerial code.

The inquiry was taking place in a cavernous room in Elizabeth Street that resembled a courtroom, but ICAC isn't a court. It's more of an inquisition, designed to root out corruption and graft in the state.

It was a pretty dry start. ICAC's counsel assisting, Scott Robertson, kicked off proceedings at 9.30 a.m., by asserting he'd be done by lunchtime. There was a short tribute to David Ipp, the legendary former ICAC commissioner who'd recently passed away. A handful of journalists listened in, but we weren't expecting much.

Then Gladys Berejiklian took the stand. Assistant commissioner Ruth McColl made her entrance shortly afterwards. McColl was a slight figure, but she loomed over the hearing from her elevated position at the apex of the room. Berejiklian swore on the Bible that she would tell the truth, and the counsel assisting then ran through the usual procedural niceties. Robertson is a droll speaker who, at times, could easily be mistaken for a funeral director. He sounded almost sleepy when, seemingly out of the blue, he asked Berejiklian whether she had ever been in a close personal relationship with Daryl Maguire.

In the ranks of journos, we pricked up our ears. Had we misheard? Berejiklian shifted in her seat before drifting off into a little speech about her friendship with the country MP. She was gently pulled back on course by the assistant commissioner, and eventually responded, yes, the friendship had developed into a close personal relationship.

'Close personal relationship.' Three bland words that, when strung together in the context of the premier's love life, were politically combustible.

To many of those inside the hearing room, this information came as little surprise. The commission's staff had known this was coming. Investigators had been reviewing tapes of Daryl Maguire and Gladys Berejiklian's phone conversations for more than three years, since as early as August 2017. But among the reporters and outside the room, there was an explosion of activity. Text messages whizzed out to and between Berejiklian's parliamentary colleagues. There was disbelief and confusion. News editors scuttled the next day's front pages. They knew this was going to be the news for the next week.

Robertson's droll tone suddenly shifted into a higher gear. What occurred over the next five hours was a grilling of the premier of an intensity that none of us had ever seen before. Even at her most vulnerable, Berejiklian gave little away. When tough questions came her way, her jaw tightened and her mouth pursed, but little more. There was no obvious tell, no lashing out. But what emerged stunned us.

Not only had Berejiklian been in a relationship with Maguire since at least 2015, she had continued to communicate with him after he was first embroiled in a separate corruption inquiry back in 2018. Not only that, but she continued to speak to him after she sacked him. It was only after she'd been called to give evidence at the ICAC inquiry into his affairs just two months earlier, on 16 August, that she'd finally ended her contact with Maguire. The last conversation they'd had was mere weeks before the public hearing she was now participating in. And yet she had never—not once—declared the relationship to anyone in government. She claimed she never had because she thought it was not of sufficient status.

Robertson's questioning focused on the premier's knowledge of Maguire's dealings with property developers, his discussions of his business dealings with her, and a jaunt he took to China. It was a forensic examination that was designed to test Berejiklian's state of mind, and it was gruelling to watch. Page after page of text messages between the pair was tabled. Maguire called Berejiklian 'Hokis', which she explained was an Armenian term of endearment. She winced as phone intercepts of their conversations were played. There was a crucial exchange where she said of one of his dealings, 'I don't need to know about that.' She wasn't paying attention anyway, she testified, adding that he was always talking about things that never eventuated.

As soon as the hearing ended, Berejiklian strode outside for a press conference that was packed with journalists clamouring for answers.[1] Phrases tumbled out of her mouth in neat soundbites: 'I stuffed up in my personal life … I trusted him for a long time and I feel really let down … There is huge separation between a personal life and public office …'

There were three themes here that would often be repeated over the next year, through to the separate inquiry into the relationship between Berejiklian and Maguire that began in late 2021. The first was the poor choices Berejiklian had made in her personal life. The question oft posed was: Who hasn't had a Daryl? It was thought none of us needed to dig terribly deep to find one.

The second was that this was a personal matter. It didn't matter that they were colleagues. It didn't matter that she was the most powerful politician in the state. It didn't matter that Maguire had to seek approval from the premier to undertake business activities outside parliament. This was personal. Nothing more.

And the third was that Berejiklian saw and heard nothing. There was no lightbulb moment, no sign of danger, no sudden stirring of suspicion that Maguire was up to no good. She trusted him, she'd said. What more was there to say?

At the press conference, Berejiklian stood aside to allow Dominic Perrottet, the then NSW treasurer and deputy leader, to talk. He backed her up, as did health minister Brad Hazzard: she had integrity, honesty, was outstanding, brilliant. It was a united front. We were reminded that she'd been our saviour through COVID-19, bushfires and floods. And in some respects, she had been. As natural disasters had struck Australia and COVID-19 had ravaged many parts of the world, Berejiklian stood out as a leader who rose to these challenges, who calmed an uneasy state in times of great crisis.

The gallery then began with their questions: Will you resign? How can you remain premier? Why didn't you report this? Berejiklian answered each one cautiously, in measured words. She never strayed far from what she'd told the inquiry. Press conferences were her dominion, after all, and she could stand her ground without the ICAC assistant commissioner hovering over her.

Eventually the presser ended, but there was a hunger for more answers. The next day, at another press conference at the NSW Parliament, Berejiklian was peppered with more questions. She was prickly this time. Her hands were clasped in front of her, conveying the distinct impression that she was annoyed. Apparently we journalists had had our fun, and pushing it further would be poor form.

A mere association with a character like Maguire easily would have toppled lesser parliamentarians. But Berejiklian was no ordinary politician. When the news about Gladys and Daryl first surfaced, New South Wales was on top of the world. As the pandemic continued to sweep across the world, the state was, against all the odds, open for business. Masks were barely in sight. Restrictions were being eased on a weekly basis. Contact tracers were working hard to contain small outbreaks. It was our little hermit paradise. We all marvelled at just how successful we were. And Gladys Berejiklian rode high on this. Like other state premiers, she had reached what had previously been an unthinkable level of celebrity for a state leader. People asked her for selfies on the street. In a political party dominated by men, and rife with allegations of the bullying and harassment of women, Berejiklian's rise to the top made her a role model for many women in politics—and plenty outside it as well.

Berejiklian had no intention of being bowled over by her dud ex-boyfriend. She and her team devised a remarkable plan of attack, a new strategy. She went on a tour of sympathetic media outlets, sharing more than she had ever shared before.

'I loved him … but I'll never speak to him again' was splashed across the front page of *The Daily Telegraph* that weekend, accompanied by a picture of Berejiklian along with the revealing admission that she had once hoped to marry Maguire.

She gave 2GB's Ben Fordham, an outspoken ally—and friend—her first broadcast interview. It 'wasn't a normal relationship', she told Fordham. She said she continued the relationship even after sacking Maguire in 2018 because he was in a dark place, and 'I didn't think I could just not continue to be his friend'.

On and on it went. And it was working. For the most part, the press gallery was with her. The internet was with her too. Hundreds of hilarious memes bounced across Instagram, TikTok and Facebook about 'Hot Mess Gladys'. They were laughing *with* her, not at her. The talkback hosts were also with her. Fordham proclaimed: 'I think we would be mad to sacrifice the best premier we've had in so long over something like this.' For another year, Berejiklian held her ground. But despite these efforts, she would eventually become the third NSW premier to resign at the feet of a body that most know simply by its acronym.

There's no question that Berejiklian had powerful advocates in government and in Sydney's cosy media scene. They played a vital role in shoring up support.

And the tactics the premier deployed to silence critics, rarely discussed publicly, were intense. But it would be a mistake to assume that the championing of Berejiklian ended there. There was—and still is—genuine, heartfelt support for her in the community, particularly from women, all over the state. A Resolve poll published in November 2021, just a month after Berejiklian's resignation as premier and amidst a second round of damaging revelations by ICAC, found that her temporarily dented popularity had bounced back to what it had been before she'd relinquished her leadership of the state. More than 40 per cent of those surveyed believed she shouldn't have stepped down as premier.[2] These figures were remarkable. Rarely had a leader in Australia been so mired in scandal yet continued to attract such approval.

This revealed a great deal about this particular era of Australian politics. Berejiklian's political demise came at a time when Australia's federal parliament was beset by scandals, some involving the use of public funds, others involving serious allegations concerning men in powerful positions abusing their power. It's easy to understand the sentiment voiced by many voters that something was deeply amiss when a powerful female leader could be brought undone by a scandal like this, but men in power in the federal system could not. It was clear that this parallel failure of scrutiny and accountability had fuelled a sense of loss and anger among voters.

Berejiklian remained popular because, in spite of a party that demoralised and let down some of its own rising stars, she had succeeded. And her crucial decision to lie about her relationship—and to continue to lie about it for years—could be forgiven by some. The same structural failures that had long diminished women in Australian politics—and which have been extensively explored in recent years— could easily be seen as having forced Berejiklian into a position where she kept a secret that she never should have kept.

Tougher questions were raised around how much the public would tolerate when it came to failures of integrity and the use of taxpayer funds. A key set of allegations related to Berejiklian's use of grant funding. The last Coalition government spent billions in taxpayer funds across a range of programs, and we now know, thanks to a series of audits, that in some cases the money was used to try and shore up the Coalition's political fortunes. Some of those schemes involved a staggeringly inappropriate use of taxpayer dollars. But much of what Gladys Berejiklian engaged in on this front had become accepted, entrenched political practice. We know this because she said as much, repeatedly, when giving evidence to ICAC.

Scott Morrison's attempts to elevate Berejiklian and admonish the work of the anti-corruption agency in the lead-up to the May 2022 federal election—such as standing up in parliament and calling ICAC a kangaroo court—showed that he was banking on voters accepting this kind of conduct as simply the cost of democracy. But his attacks on the commission, and his attempts to link his political fortunes to Berejiklian, were badly misjudged. It turned out that while some voters certainly did like Gladys, integrity was an issue at the forefront their minds. It's now clear that honesty, along with climate change, was a dominant and decisive issue in the many key federal seats where moderate Liberal candidates were wiped out by the teal wave. Gladys Berejiklian's name was no help to Morrison then.

This long saga unfolded publicly for more than four years. It emerged in dribs and drabs of coverage: a phone call here, a text message there. People understandably asked: What did she really do? Ignored a few red flags from her dodgy boyfriend and helped out a shooting club with some grant funding? So what?

But this one mistake, this one lie, about a very personal matter, snowballed into a series of bigger lies. It clouded Berejiklian's judgement and coopted the extraordinary powers of a state premier. It revealed the darker side of a premier who had banked on an image that was overwhelmingly respectful and polite and honest. What ICAC eventually uncovered was just how brittle that image was.

~

He called himself 'Daryl the builder'. Nobody else did. Daryl Maguire was the country boy from Wagga Wagga, known to locals simply as 'Wagga', who saw himself as the regional town's saviour. Anything they needed, he could get. When he first spoke in the NSW Parliament after winning his seat in 1999, he professed his great love for the town. 'I am captivated by its beauty, blinded by its potential and passionate for its cause and its people,' he told the chamber with a trademark blend of energy and passion.

The town and its residents were Maguire's home. He knew them, and they knew him. His father was an illiterate drover who travelled 160 kilometres every day taking Maguire and his sister to and from school. Maguire's life was forged in the tough lessons he learnt from his father. So went the myth he made for himself.

He bought a horse agistment farm, which sat next to the house he shared with his two children and his wife, Maureen. He was determined to make his mark. And pursuing money for his electorate was one of the great callings he saw for himself. In his maiden speech, he went on to mention regional jobs funding and the local Wagga base hospital. 'Put these items on your to-do list, minister,' he said, 'because I will pester you until I get what I want.'

And he pestered relentlessly. He was constantly at the doors of state ministers, asking for handouts for the electorate. In one video from 2016, the tall country man, accompanied by arts minister Don Harwin, sported his trademark open-collared shirt and akubra while announcing more arts funding. He cheerfully whirled around at the end of the press conference, saying: 'Thanks for the money!'

Maguire was generally thought of as occasionally charming but mostly useless. While he thought of himself as Daryl the builder, behind his back, plenty of people in Wagga called him by another name: 'Do-Little Daryl'.

He was also an outrageous flirt. John Larter, a Liberal councillor in Tumut, recalls him always bringing wine to the women's branch of the Wagga Liberal Party. It was an effort to prop up Maguire's preselection chances. 'He'd go and have cups of tea and scones and endear himself to everyone. But the reality was, there were two sides to Daryl Maguire,' Larter tells me.

There was something undeniably appealing about Maguire. His ability to saunter into a room, to strike up a conversation with anyone about anything, was real. He had charisma. But money was always on his mind, and not just for his electorate. He was obsessed with his own wealth, always scheming, always hustling.

It's difficult to know exactly when that conniving crossed a line into something more sinister. But at some point, Daryl Maguire began operating in a very different way. He began to see his parliamentary office as a vehicle for personal wealth. The schemes were endless. Strange figures were continually entering and exiting his office. Money kept changing hands—not all of it was dirty, but plenty of it was. There was cash for visa schemes, property development commissions. And it was all run out of his political office.

The problem was, he was bad at being corrupt. Comically bad. He was the George Costanza of political grifting. Daryl had grand designs, yet somehow they never quite came to fruition. Still, he complained endlessly about his debts, and his machinations became more brazen.

In 2018, the country watched Do-Little Daryl suddenly turn into 'Dodgy Daryl'. The Wagga politician found his voice played out loud for the world to hear in a series of telephone intercepts. 'My client is mega big,' looking for a 'quick' sale, and he didn't want to fuck around, he was captured saying.

It wasn't pleasant. This was the other side of Maguire that Larter refers to. A meaner, harsher Daryl who rarely made his way into the public domain. Stories rapidly emerged about the MP's abusive behaviour: his rants at staffers, his blow-ups at party members. There was an ugliness to it, a meanness. He resigned first from the Liberal Party and then shortly afterwards from parliament.

Back in 1999, Maguire ended his maiden speech in parliament with these words:

> I have been taught to be honest, have respect, work hard, be tenacious, and never give up. I have been taught that one's word is one's bond and that I must earn people's trust.[3]

Almost all of this was a lie. We now know that Maguire was not honest. He did not respect people. He did not work hard—or if he did, it was only for himself. But he was tenacious, and he was very good at earning the trust of those around him. One of the people whose trust he earned was Gladys Berejiklian.

~

When she was NSW premier, one of the many ordinary things we discovered about Gladys Berejiklian was that she ate Cheds crackers for breakfast. This fact emerged after much furious attention was paid to her biscuit selection as she strode out the door of her North Sydney home, crackers in hand, suit jacket on. She was always on the move, didn't have time to eat. She was busy running the state. Many versions of this story were told over the years. It was one of her defining characteristics. She worked hard, wasn't flashy. She drank Coke with no sugar.

Berejiklian was the daughter of Armenian migrants, one of the many diasporas represented in Australia. Arriving in Australia at the age of five, she didn't speak a word of English. But she learnt fast. It was a remarkable success story that resonated with many. It resonates with me—my mother arrived in Australia from Egypt at age five. Every migrant family can relate to this, and understand what it means to see someone with such an ordinary story find power.

Berejiklian was not ordinary, though. Far from it. She was an extraordinary politician. She was active in student politics and became a fixture in the NSW Young Liberals when she was at university, rising to president in 1996. She was then preselected for the seat of Willoughby in North Sydney and won at the 2003 state election, albeit by a slim margin. She was appointed shadow transport minister in 2006, and when the Liberal Party regained government under Barry O'Farrell in 2011, she became the serving transport minister.

At the time, transportation in New South Wales was viewed by many in politics as a poisoned chalice. The state's rail and road system seemed an unfathomable mess to most. But Berejiklian dominated the area. She got the trains to work, she built things. She was prepared, on top of her brief. This was more than anyone could say about the twilight years of the previous state Labor government, which were marred by dysfunction and corruption.

She quickly rose through the Cabinet ranks to treasurer. When Mike Baird resigned, she became his unlikely successor, in January 2017. There was a good deal of uncertainty about how she would be seen by the electorate, but those doubts were vanquished at the 2019 state election. Her government was returned to power for a third term, the first time the incumbent had done so in almost fifty years. Berejiklian also became the first female premier in New South Wales to prevail at a general election.

Her rise to power was aided by the backing of powerful figures in the party. One vocal source of support was powerbroker-turned-lobbyist Michael Photios, who wrote in *The Australian* that the young Armenian Australian from Ryde had 'emerged a

Labor dragon slayer'.[4] In the quagmire of factional politics that was the Liberal Party, Berejiklian was part of what was loosely described as the moderate faction. And a key ally of that faction was Photios, who for some years was simultaneously its chairman and head of the powerful lobbyist firm PremierState. In February 2017, in what was reported as a decision made in part to curb attacks on Berejiklian's links to Photios, he resigned from the chairmanship, but his lobbying work continued.

After the 2019 election, Berejiklian's government went from strength to strength, with the premier shining in moments of crisis. Perhaps her greatest moment came during the 2019–20 summer bushfire season. When prime minister Scott Morrison disappeared for a family holiday to Hawaii, Berejiklian was the one calming New South Wales as black clouds blanketed the state.

She was a disarming operator. After interviews with journalists, she would chat with them, and with the camera crew. She would ask about their wives, husbands, children, whether they were single. Many walked away with the feeling that she was really interested in them. But she always remained unequivocally private. She had no children and no obvious partner. While single men in politics were rarely asked about their personal lives, journalists persistently hassled

Berejiklian about hers. She batted their questions away with deft ease, but those questions lingered.

It was in the early 2010s that Gladys Berejiklian and Daryl Maguire found themselves growing closer. Both were longtime political allies who shared the same mentor, former premier Barry O'Farrell. Sometime around 2014, the two began a personal relationship, when Berejiklian was transport minister. They kept it a secret. Berejiklian told no-one—not her parliamentary colleagues, not her friends, not even her family. There are dozens of videos of the two of them making announcements in Wagga over these years. Watching them closely for any hint of the connection between them, there really is nothing there. There is no lingering glance, rather they avert their eyes. And they rarely smile at each other. There is no visible warmth between them.

Staffers in Berejiklian's office recall many occasions when Maguire would upset someone. He had a bad habit of shouting at junior staffers. Sometimes Berejiklian would be briefed on this by her team, along with some blunt assessments of Maguire's character. They recount her listening closely, with sympathy, and assuring them it would be dealt with. So when those staffers learnt of the pair's secret, they were shocked by the level of deception. The premier's own chief of staff, Sarah Cruickshank, held Maguire in poor standing.

We still don't have a full picture of the relationship between the premier and the MP. But from the snippets offered by the telephone intercepts played during the ICAC hearings, you can discern clues about the dynamic they shared.

In a call which took place on 5 September 2017, one of many conversations in which Maguire talked about making money, he told Berejiklian that she 'Didn't ask me how much money I got back'. She replied that it was 'because you'd swear at me'. He then told her he wouldn't, but added: 'It's only when you want me to spend money that I swear.' Such exchanges revealed a weak man, a man who was deeply insecure about his ability to provide for Berejiklian, a powerful woman on a vastly superior salary and who was, effectively, his boss.

The very first exchange between Maguire and Berejiklian that was intercepted by ICAC and publicly revealed dates from 1 August 2017. It set the tone for their future chats. Maguire fretted about how he wouldn't have any money unless he could 'pull off these deals'. Berejiklian pleaded with him not to worry, telling him she could support herself, that he should just do whatever he needed to for himself and his kids. He replied: 'Yeah, but beats tripping around and stuff.' She also urged him to stay healthy. He told her how the 'blokes working on the farm' couldn't believe how healthy he was. 'I outwork them, they can't believe it,' he said.

It was the kind of sprawling brag you might expect from Donald Trump. It exposed a pitiful figure who, now firmly in middle age, was desperately trying to stay relevant. He was obsessed with legacy building, keen to build roads, bridges and towers, to make Wagga the greatest city on Earth. But he could only accomplish that with the help of Berejiklian, who wielded the real power.

And so, over many years, he began to lean harder on her, to work her, to ask her for more and more.

~

It was August 2017 and Daryl Maguire was going to China. And Niall Blair, the then trade minister, was not happy about it.

Blair, a respected Nationals minister, had been planning his first trade delegation in his ministerial role, which would visit Shanghai. Maguire had recently approached Blair's office about a Mascot-based exporting company called United World Enterprises (UWE), raising it with one of Blair's senior advisers, Charlie Cull. UWE was an export business that specialised in moving a range of products from Australia to China, and while it initially focused on more niche goods like textiles and cosmetics, it eventually broadened its dealings to include products like wheat and beef. It was unusual for backbench state MPs to get involved in a trade delegation, so Cull was surprised by the approach. But he knew that from time to time, MPs did have to deal with trade-related issues that came up within their electorates, so he agreed to meet with Maguire to discuss it further.

It was an odd meeting. Cull felt that Maguire was promoting UWE, advocating for it, in an unusually intense way. Maguire seemed to be claiming there were local jobs on the line in his electorate. What Maguire hadn't told Cull was that he was secretly trying to gain a position on UWE's board, once again acting in his own interests, not in the interests of his electorate. Maguire walked away from the meeting with Cull feeling dissatisfied. Days later, Cull learnt that Maguire was planning on visiting China at the same time as Blair, effectively gatecrashing the minister's inaugural mission.

Maguire did not have a reputation for diplomacy. In fact, he was more renowned on Macquarie Street for throwing tantrums at government ministers when things didn't go his way. Mixing him and China's political elite didn't seem like a good idea. Blair feared Maguire's trip could cause a diplomatic incident, embarrassing the minister and more broadly

New South Wales. So his staff contacted Berejiklian's office. Sarah Cruickshank promised to talk Maguire down, then informed Berejiklian she was going to have a discrete chat with the Wagga MP. Maguire would learn this call was coming, because Berejiklian would tip him off.

On 30 August, Berejiklian called Maguire and asked, 'Did Sarah ring you from my office?'

'No, why?' Maguire responded.

Berejiklian explained that Niall Blair had called to say, 'Tell Daryl not to worry, I'm raising the [local jobs] issue on his behalf in China.'

Maguire pushed back, saying he didn't believe anything would be done about it: 'So what they're frightened of is … that he's gonna have a round table so they've invited all these people, [to] shake hands and suck dicks, right.'

Berejiklian replied: 'And they seem to think it's in your electorate. I didn't say anything.'

The call ended with another absurd boast from Maguire, that he had met Xi Jinping, and Cruickshank hadn't.

~

After Gladys Berejiklian's first appearance at ICAC in October 2020, where calls like those described above were played, obvious questions were raised about whether, at any point, the premier had created a conflict of interest in exercising her public duties and simultaneously conducting a private relationship with Maguire.

Over the last two years, we've seen a deluge of grant programs come under fire at both the federal and state levels. The concerns around these schemes fundamentally boil down to one thing: that taxpayer funds should not be used for political purposes. And yet that's exactly what has happened time and time again. Sports rorts, community safety rorts, car park rorts: it's as if an endless number of schemes have been usurped for political purposes.

Berejiklian was swept up in one of these grant scandals around the same time it was revealed she was in a relationship with Daryl Maguire. A $140 million community grant program involving local councils was under major political fire. The money had been dished out without any due process being followed, with most of the funds going to Coalition-led councils. It was unclear who exactly had made these decisions. What was clear was that a staffer in Berejiklian's office had swiftly shredded a series of documents outlining the premier's 'approval' of certain grants. It appeared to be a case of brazen pork-barrelling, and Berejiklian was right in the middle of it.

True to form, she never went to ground. Instead, she went right at the issue, proclaiming in a November 2020 press conference that pork-barrelling was in fact something the electorate expected:

> It's not something the community likes … but it's an accusation I will wear … It's not unique to our government … It's not an illegal practice. Unfortunately it does happen from time to time by every government.[5]

The comments were a rare admission of how an increasing number of senior politicians seemed to view the public purse. Pork-barrelling was not only business-as-usual, it was expected. According to this vision of the world, the public understood that by voting in a particular way, they would benefit the most.

I worked up a report on this topic in October 2020 for the ABC current affairs program *7.30*, covering it at the same time as lots of other news organisations were. Berejiklian's media advisers were unhappy with our account of the grant program. One of them called me up the day after the program had aired and said, 'You made it look dodgy. You made it look like something was inappropriate.'

I asked if she had factual issues she wanted to raise, but she couldn't point to any. The adviser then paused for a moment before indicating that her office had a very good relationship with *7.30*, and with then-presenter Leigh Sales. 'It would be a shame if your reporting jeopardised that,' she said.

Was this a warning shot? Media advisers sometimes think they can pit the interests of different parts of news organisations against each other. (The staffer recently told me they don't recall making these specific comments, but acknowledged a 'difference of opinion at the time'. They said I hadn't correctly interpreted the conversation, and pointed out that Berejiklian later participated in interviews with Sales.)

If it was a tactic, it might have worked elsewhere, but not at *7.30*. All it did was spark the first glimmer of an idea, which is how lots of stories start. This idea was simple and took the form of a question: had Gladys Berejiklian been involved in awarding any grants that Daryl Maguire might have benefited from?

Eventually, this would take us to a dinky shooting association in Wagga that would become a key focus of ICAC's corruption inquiry.

~

The ICAC investigation into Maguire wrapped up at the end of 2020. The commission put out a timetable for submissions, and all indications were that everything would soon be tidied up. Berejiklian and her colleagues thought she had weathered the crisis. But that wouldn't be the case.

During the inquiry, investigators had focused on the business dealings of Maguire, in particular those involving a company called G8way International,[6] and on whether he had used his position in public office for private benefit. Maguire admitted that he had secretly directed G8way with his business partner, Phil Elliott. According to Elliott's evidence to ICAC, Maguire suggested to the then CEO of the Australian Clay Target Association in Wagga, Tony Turner, that he contact Elliott about purchasing chairs for a convention centre from China. Elliott told the inquiry that G8way expected to make a small commission on the deal. Of course, through his interest in the company, Maguire stood to profit from the deal too.

Almost as an afterthought, towards the end of the public hearings, Scott Robertson tabled an exhibit that he casually described as 'other dealings' of Maguire. Inside were thousands of pages of interviews, records and emails. It looked like the bits that ICAC thought might be worth looking into, but they either weren't sure or didn't have the resources to investigate.

An important part of journalism that is rarely discussed is the many hours spent reading boring, droll, bureaucratic documents filled with almost nothing of interest. Sometimes you can dig for hours, even days, and come up for air with absolutely nothing. My *7.30* colleague Alex McDonald and I spent weeks poring over those documents. There were tantalising glimpses of other dealings Maguire had attempted to embark on: a pilot school he'd tried to partner with, wineries, all sorts of other ventures. But none of them really led anywhere. Alex and I started wondering, if ICAC wasn't that interested in them, was there really any point in continuing to go through them?

Things changed when we found, buried in the exhibit, an interview that an ICAC investigator had conducted with Turner. It revealed that the purchase of the chairs was linked to a development that was largely bankrolled by the NSW Government. There was also a curious reference to a government min-ister getting involved in the process. It turned out that the grant funding had followed a highly unusual process. An announcement was made by Maguire in January 2017 concerning $5.5 million in funding, but months later, the club had not yet received any formal paperwork.[7] 'It was really scant in detail, to be honest,' Turner told the ICAC investigator. 'I mean, I'm sitting there in February and March, April, May, without any signed documents. An announcement was made that we'd been given the $5.5 million, and I received nothing else after that.'

And that wasn't all. The shooting organisation had actually sought a small amount of funding for a much more modest proposal. But out of the blue, Turner had received a phone call from a government official saying that an unidentified government minister 'wants it bigger'. It was a peculiar comment, one that seemed worth exploring further—especially as, at the time of the first hearing, ICAC was focused on Maguire's conduct, not on Berejiklian's.

After weeks of digging, it became clear that Berejiklian had been involved in the administration of this grant. There were subtle signs that she had played a role at various points. Critically, we learnt that the premier had participated in a Cabinet meeting to secure the funding in December 2016.

Eventually, in December 2020, two months after Berejiklian's appearance at ICAC, Alex and I produced a story for *7.30* outlining the strange circumstances of this grant and the premier's potential role in it. She responded by denying there was any conflict. The story bubbled away for twenty-four hours and then vanished, as these kinds of stories often do.

Many had assumed that Berejiklian's first appearance at ICAC would be her last. She had succeeded in persuading a good deal of the public, and her factional allies in the party, that she could still continue in the job of premier. But a few days after our program aired, ICAC announced it was taking 'further investigative steps'. They were very interested in what we had uncovered.

~

It was Monday 9 August 2021 and Sydney was deep in the Delta outbreak, with cases averaging more than one thousand a day. There was a sense of panic, anger and despair. Gladys Berejiklian's daily press conferences were a hallmark of those strange times. She and other state premiers became rock stars of the pandemic. The conferences were essential viewing. A macabre sense of dread was prompted when the case numbers were read out, but Berejiklian soon became a figure of immense comfort to millions across the state. For many of us, it was reassuring to see her appear on our screens every morning.

I caught a taxi to the premier's press conference that morning on the ground floor of the offices of NSW Health in North Sydney, happy to get out of my house. I had no intention of asking about COVID-19, though. I wanted to ask about Daryl Maguire. When my taxi pulled up, one of the premier's minders clocked my arrival and sent off a quick message to a colleague.

A few days earlier, I had sent twenty detailed questions to the premier about her role in awarding

GLADYS: A LEADER'S UNDOING

the Clay Target Association grant to Maguire. I knew that ICAC was looking at it. I knew they were seeking documents about the grant. Quiet discussions were being held behind the scenes as senior bureaucrats and a handful of politicians became aware of these requests. It all pointed to the commission tightening its investigative scope, and potentially focusing on Berejiklian personally.

The premier's office declined to respond on the record to a single question, offering only a short 'background' statement. It was an increasingly common tactic media advisers deployed on behalf of their political masters, to put statements on 'background', refusing to place them on the record. It meant that, by convention, the statement couldn't be explicitly used by a journalist. The politician was free to say whatever they wanted, the intention of which was sometimes simply to plant a seed of doubt in the mind of a journalist. So I decided to go down and ask Berejiklian some of the questions in person.

I joined the handful of reporters at the presser. One journalist I greeted asked if I was planning to question the premier about Daryl Maguire. I said I was. Sky News political correspondent Andrew Clennell overheard our conversation and whirled around. 'You've got absolutely no chance today mate,' he told me. 'There aren't going to be any questions on anything else,' by which he meant anything other than COVID.

Clennell wasn't being bullish. He was giving a frank and sceptical assessment of the way in which these press conferences were managed. They were highly staged and managed events. When politicians did not want to answer questions, they would find a way not to. They were also very tribal affairs. There was just a handful of full-time reporters in the state press gallery. They were all vaguely competitive, and they all knew each other. Interlopers were rarely greeted with much enthusiasm, and I was very much an interloper on their turf.

Berejiklian walked up to the podium, flanked by Brad Hazzard and NSW Chief Health Officer Kerry Chant. An emergency doctor had been invited to talk to the public, and we heard from him first. Then it was time for some questions. Clennell tried to jump in to ask the premier something, but a media adviser shouted back, 'Questions for the doctor first.' Clennell muttered 'Come on' under his breath.

At these press conferences, politicians generally prefer queries about a set topic initially, so asking something you know a politician will not like has to be delicately timed. About half an hour after the questions finally opened up to Berejiklian and Chant, I sensed an opportunity. Berejiklian was standing in a corner of the room while Chant was speaking. I took a step forward and asked her why she'd intervened in a $5.5 million grant Maguire was pursuing. Wasn't that a serious conflict of interest?

Berejiklian's face dropped like an anchor. She stalked back to the microphones, shooing me off. 'Can you stand back please?' she snapped. I was already standing metres away from her but I couldn't help but respond, instinctively jumping back and nearly crashing into another reporter. I could practically feel the gazes of her media advisers, all of them presumably wishing my head would explode or that I would spontaneously combust on the spot.

Berejiklian batted away my question by saying, 'All the proper processes were followed.' She then looked around the room, as if desperately trying to find another reporter to lock eyes with. I tried again, clamouring to be heard from under my mask, and managed to punch through the ambient shouts of other journalists asking about COVID-19. 'We've seen the letters,' I said, 'You thanked Maguire for bringing it to the government's attention. Wasn't it a serious conflict of interest to get involved at all in this grant given you were in a relationship at the time?'

She turned back to me, incredulous that I had dared to raise the issue again. Her face was dark and furious. She practically snarled at me: 'I refer you to my previous answer and please respect this press conference.'

It was a brutal and decisive end to the exchange. She turned away, and the questioning shifted back to COVID. No-one else asked about the grant. A short time later, Berejiklian ended the press conference.

Soon, my inbox was filled with messages reflecting two different perceptions of the incident. Some people claimed that it was wildly inappropriate for me to even deign to ask about anything other than COVID-19 in the midst of our state's great crisis. But others were appalled at the premier's response. They'd had a glimpse of something harsh, a moment—just a moment—when Berejiklian had let her disciplined veneer slip. It appeared to expose a politician who seemed not just angry but perhaps, quite surprisingly, a little frightened.

Bubbling away beneath the confrontation at the press conference was something that Berejiklian was deeply worried about. We knew that ICAC had issued notices to obtain documents relating to the Clay Target Association, tied not just to Maguire but to other individuals linked to the club. A handful of senior public servants had also been called to give evidence in March and April that year, behind closed doors. Rumours had even begun to circulate that the deputy premier, John Barilaro, had also been called in as a witness. They were all sworn to secrecy, of course, but with ICAC poking around government agencies, word got around. Some in the Liberal Party were hearing increasing murmurs that the corruption agency was focusing its inquiries on this one particular grant.

Berejiklian knew that journalists knew that ICAC was looking at this issue, so her fury was understandable. She had worked hard over the past year to contain the fallout from the corruption probe, and limit the damage to her. In the process, she had courted countless journalists. And yet here was some nobody from the ABC banging on about grants!

What struck me about the exchange was her use of the word 'respect'. How were you supposed to respect a press conference? It was a strange response, but I think what Berejiklian was getting at is that I wasn't playing by the rules she had drawn up for how these events should work. Unfortunately, too many journalists in New South Wales had adhered to these rules, and done so willingly. At their heart was a thin line of acceptability corralling what kinds of questions you could ask and when you could ask them. When reporters tried to push past that line, they were punished or ostracised. It had been clear for some time that Berejiklian was not willing to engage with questions about Maguire or the corruption probe.

All the while, as most of Sydney remained locked down because of the pandemic, ICAC continued to do its work.

~

Behind the scenes, ICAC's investigation had reached a crucial point. Investigators had determined they had enough evidence for, and had satisfied the standards required to hold, a public inquiry into Gladys Berejiklian. They called Berejiklian in for what is legally termed a private examination in September 2021. At this point, there would have been little doubt in her mind they were exploring aspects of her conduct.

In the depths of Sydney's lockdown, ICAC's three permanent commissioners had secretly met to consider the evidence that investigators had gathered. The introduction of three commissioners was part of a series of reforms initiated by the NSW Government in 2016. It was designed to ensure a check on ICAC's power. No single commissioner could make a decision alone—they had to make their decisions together. In Gladys Berejiklian's case, it was unanimous. The triumvirate agreed that there was sufficient public interest to hold an inquiry into Berejiklian's conduct. Their concerns fell into two broad categories: her knowledge of Maguire's dealings, and her role in awarding grants and whether, in doing so, she had breached public trust.

On the morning of 30 September 2021, ICAC issued a media statement advising they were now investigating Berejiklian herself. The focus was her potential failure to disclose Maguire's conduct, and whether she encouraged or induced it, as well as her own conduct in awarding both the $5.5 million Clay Target Association grant and a $20 million contribution to the Riverina Conservatorium of Music, also based in Wagga. What some of Berejiklian's colleagues in the Liberal Party had for months feared would happen, had finally happened. Public speculation immediately turned to what Berejiklian would do now.

The night before the announcement, Berejiklian, who'd been made aware of what was about to happen, met with her staff, her lawyers and senior members of the government. They agonised over what to do. Her barrister, Bret Walker, advised that, at least legally, she could continue to serve in parliament if she stood aside as premier. Apparently ashen-faced, she called a press conference to coincide with ICAC's statement.

The following morning, Berejiklian walked briskly to the podium and said that with great reluctance, she had made a difficult decision. She raced through it all, many of the matters already subject to attacks by opposition parliamentarians. But she wanted to make it clear she had always acted with the highest level of integrity. She had always asserted, she said, that if her own ministers were under investigation by an integrity or anti-corruption agency, they would need to stand aside while that investigation occurred. Indeed, in September 2019, Berejiklian had asked John Sidoti, her then minister for sport, multiculturalism, seniors and veterans, to relinquish his ministerial duties when ICAC announced it was examining his behaviour. It appeared, at least for the moment, that Berejiklian herself would do just this—stand down as premier, but fight on in parliament.

But in an extraordinary move, Berejiklian went far further. Not only was she stepping down as premier, she was also resigning from parliament. The people of the state needed certainty, she said.

Gladys Berejiklian's self-ejection from the NSW Parliament stunned her colleagues, who just weeks earlier had been assured by her that she was on solid ground. She explained to the press gathered in front of her:

> Resigning at this time is against every instinct in my being and something which I do not want to do. I love my job and I love serving the community. But I have been given no option following the statement that's been issued today.[8]

She also lashed out at ICAC, deriding the timing of the commission's investigation, in a critical period of the pandemic, when New South Wales was uneasily emerging from lockdown. She said she regretted being unable to see the state through to a return to normal life, and thanked all the frontline workers. She'd given it her all, she said, telling people to stay safe.

All up, Berejiklian's statement lasted just six minutes. In those six minutes, the NSW Government was shattered, forced to remake itself.

~

When former NSW premier Mike Baird appeared at the ICAC hearing in October 2021, he seemed smaller, diminished. The usually charismatic Baird had left politics behind when Berejiklian succeeded him as premier in January 2017. But the charm was now gone. In the hearing room, he was grim-faced and stony. He spoke so softly that the assistant commissioner asked him to raise his voice.

Baird was a reluctant witness. Berejiklian had been a friend and ally for a long time, and Baird had always known her as a person of great integrity. Giving evidence at an investigation into Berejiklian was something he'd never anticipated doing. It was the last place he'd expected to be.

It was only a few days into the inquiry into Berejiklian, but a pattern had already begun to emerge. Every official and member of government who appeared was asked two critical questions: 'Do you think Gladys Berejiklian should have disclosed her relationship with Mr Maguire?' and 'Would you have acted differently if you were aware of it?'

ICAC was attempting to build a parallel world where Berejiklian had disclosed her relationship with the Wagga MP. It was doing so in order to ascertain whether people in key positions would have acted differently in the awarding of taxpayer funds. A crucial hypothetical was how this would have affected the December 2016 Expenditure Review Committee meeting at which the Clay Target Association grant was approved. A standing order had asked the committee members whether they had any conflicts to declare. Berejiklian had remained silent.

Baird told the inquiry that when he learnt about Berejiklian and Maguire's relationship, he was 'incredulous'. When he was asked whether knowledge of that association would have affected anything he did as premier, Baird paused before slowly responding, 'Certainly I think it should have been disclosed.'

Everyone else who was asked this question gave the same reply: yes, the relationship should have been disclosed. And yes, had they known about it, there were things they would have done differently. It was devastating evidence for Berejiklian, particularly as there had been so many concerns about the merits of the Clay Target Association proposal.

The bureaucracy had shown vanishingly small support for this grant. Michael Toohey, Director of the Office of Sport, had been especially rankled by the way it was handled. Toohey was the very model of a public servant: diligent, hard-working and scrupulously honest. And out of all of the bureaucrats who appeared at ICAC, he was the most frank. He'd spent years helping government ministers make the right decisions when it came to allocating taxpayer funds, ensuring, in his own words, that the government didn't treat the public coffers 'like an ATM and just give money to whomever'. He had been aghast at the Clay Target Association grant.

At one point, it had been suggested that the proposed facilities would host the Invictus Games, a multisport competition for injured or sick servicemen and women. There was just one problem: there was no shooting event at the Invictus Games. And the games themselves had already been slated for Sydney. It was just one of many problems with the allocation of those funds.

Toohey finished his testimony with the observation that he was conscious people might see him as some upset bureaucrat banging on about a process no-one cared about. 'I believe that there is a value in the process,' he told the inquiry. The value was for the taxpayers, and in ensuring the government didn't find itself on the hook for millions and millions of dollars. His evidence was clear: the Wagga project was highly unusual and not one that he supported.

~

It was the morning of Friday 29 October, and Gladys Berejiklian was due to make her first appearance at the ICAC hearings. But no-one knew where she was.

At the rear entrance of the ICAC offices in Elizabeth Street, there was a growing crowd of journalists and police. A group of tradies installing a commercial kitchen had just knocked off and were also watching the spectacle, mystified about what was taking place. One news organisation had had a chopper outside Berejiklian's house for the past half-hour, but there had been no sign of her. When a call came through saying she still hadn't left her home, everyone started to relax. A moment later, a white van whizzed past—half the cameras missed it.

Gladys Berejiklian had no intention of slinking into ICAC. Her entrance was characteristically direct, marching up in a striking green jacket to address the waiting cameras. She was in control, smiling and confident, as camera crew operators jostled each other, scrambling to get a shot. 'I've always put the public first,' she said, once again stressing she had never done anything wrong, and adding that she was looking forward to giving evidence.

When Berejiklian appeared on ICAC's live feed a few minutes later—COVID restrictions kept the media and other non-essential parties out of the room—the hearings took on a surreal quality, akin to watching a reality television show unfold. Viewers were given a bird's-eye glimpse of Berejiklian seated near assistant commissioner Ruth McColl, and, due to a badly angled camera, Scott Robertson's nostrils.

A dynamic quickly emerged in the hearing. Berejiklian, forever the politician, couldn't resist a good speech. Barristers are sticklers for yes or no answers to their questions, but Berejiklian continued to duck and weave, giving a stump speech at every opportunity. Scott Robertson looked annoyed— his nostrils, still far too visible on-screen, flared noticeably. McColl increasingly sighed as she tried to reign in the reluctant witness.

Berejiklian was defiant and unrepentant when questioned about her roles in the awarding of the Clay Target Association and Riverina Conservatorium of Music grants. She did not recall having any particular interest in the fundings. She also said she had not given any special attention to Daryl Maguire's projects, claiming that he was treated no differently to any other member of her government.

This evidence was severely tested. In a phone call intercepted less than a month before Maguire's reputation was shredded at his first ICAC appearance in 2018, Berejiklian casually told him that she had secured $170 million in funding for Wagga's Base Hospital. 'I've just fixed that one,' she said. She went on to describe to Maguire how she had obtained the funding 'in five minutes' after speaking to then treasurer Dominic Perrottet: 'I just spoke to Dom and I said put the 140 [million dollars] in the budget. He just does what I ask him to.'

In another intercepted call, Berejiklian and Maguire discussed his pet project to revamp the conservatorium. Berejiklian complained about a government bureaucrat who was working on the funding proposal: 'I can't stand that guy. His head will be gone soon.'

'Not until he fixes my conservatorium,' objected Maguire.

'Alright, good,' Berejiklian responded. 'Tell him to fix it and then after he fixes it, I'm sacking him.'

Much was revealed in this crude exchange. It mirrored that glimpse of Berejiklian at the August

2021 press conference: the ruthless, calculating politician. But the toughest moments involved their relationship. The key issue was whether, under the ministerial code, Berejiklian had had an obligation to disclose her relationship with Daryl Maguire. This required the interactions between the two to meet the threshold of an intimate relationship, and ICAC laboured over this question.

A text message was presented in which Berejiklian described Maguire as 'my family'. It was put to her that this showed the significance of their relationship. What followed was a tortuous exchange where Berejiklian insisted that she hadn't really meant 'family' like her brothers or sisters, but a different sort of 'family'. It was queasily awkward watching this.

It was next revealed that, after Maguire was summoned as a witness to the ICAC inquiry in 2018, the pair had had an almost hour-long conversation in which Maguire talked about his business dealings in detail. Snippets of this were played, making Berejiklian cringe. When she was asked why she hadn't suspected Maguire was engaging in wrongdoing, she said: 'I'd known him for a long time, and I trusted him, and I trusted that if he had any private interests, and that was a matter for him, that he would disclose them.'

Berejiklian's response emphasised the word she had long deployed in her defence: 'trust'. This was the term she came back to time and time again. Trust is a feeble word in politics. All politicians know that trust has its limits: people lie all the time, motives are hidden, it's part of the business. And yet it was the crutch that Gladys Berejiklian leant on when protesting she did not know what Maguire was up to.

Berejiklian's trust in Maguire ran deep. She loved him, as he loved her. She said she had her doubts about their future, which is likely why she never introduced Maguire to her family. But her trust in him was given depth by their intimacy. That was Berejiklian's great blind spot, and it undid her argument that she hadn't needed to flag the relationship. In relation to the work of government, intimate relationships are precisely the ones that need to be disclosed.

There are a number of moments in the phone intercepts when we got to understand how well Berejiklian and Maguire knew each other. During one exchange, there was a crunching sound in the background. Berejiklian told Maguire that she knew he was at his house because she could hear the gravel. It was as though she could picture the long gravel driveway that led to Maguire's beautiful sandstone home in North Wagga Wagga. Perhaps she even recalled walking up that gravel pathway on one of her visits, after a long week in the premier's office.

The day before Berejiklian's testimony, Maguire himself had appeared at the inquiry, beaming in remotely from that very same house. Dressed in a grey suit, he looked tired and worn out, but relieved, possibly at not having to face the mob in Sydney. It was known that Daryl Maguire had a key to Berejiklian's house, and when he was asked if he'd ever returned it, he paused and looked away. It was the only time in the hearing he did this. There was a long silence, and then he said that no, he had not. It was a moment of pain that demonstrated how much he cared for her.

Berejiklian had asserted that no-one could really know how one person felt about another, except for that person themselves. But what someone says about a relationship and what they do within it are two very different things. We saw in the moments just described both a great depth of feeling and a great sense of loss.

After two gruelling days, Berejiklian left the witness box. She was visibly tired, but she still walked confidently outside for a final press conference, a last public display of defiance. There was just a handful of journalists there, including me. I stood a little more than a metre away from her, wondering if she was going to shoo me again. She glanced at me but gave away nothing. Then she launched into a familiar refrain: she had done nothing wrong, and she was looking forward to clearing her name.

I began to ask a question, but she was already walking away.

~

During the ICAC hearings, ferocious attacks were launched against the anti-corruption agency. NSW Liberals President Philip Ruddock slammed it. Former Liberal MP Pru Goward derided it. Kathryn Greiner, whose ex-husband Nick Greiner's tenure as premier had been cut short when he'd resigned due to an ICAC inquiry, sneered at it. This was a beat-up, they said, nothing more than a political hit job. For months afterwards, Berejiklian's federal Coalition allies angrily lashed out at the treatment she'd been subjected to. This was done partly out of fealty to the Liberal Party, but also for heavily political reasons—to justify the federal government dragging its heels for two years on delivering a national integrity agency to oversee politicians and the public service.

Former federal MP Jason Falinski became a regular critic of ICAC, lambasting it at every opportunity. But arguably the fiercest criticism came from then prime minister Scott Morrison. In November 2021, during the final sitting weeks of parliament for the year, he savaged ICAC under cover of parliamentary privilege. He proclaimed it a 'kangaroo court', shouting: 'The premier of New South Wales was done over by a bad process, an abuse. What was done to Gladys Berejiklian, the people of New South Wales know, was an absolute disgrace.'[9]

Certainly, no observer of ICAC could say that the commission hadn't made mistakes. For one thing, it had made a colossal error in October 2020, when it was first taking a close look at Gladys Berejiklian. The commission accidentally uploaded to the internet a confidential transcript of a private hearing. That transcript contained a great deal of deeply personal information about the relationship between Berejiklian and Maguire that was never intended to be made public. The commission swiftly moved to make a non-publication order, but the horse had bolted. Dozens of journalists and other viewers of the inquiry had already downloaded it.

It was extremely worrying that an agency with extensive powers to intercept phone calls, including the ability to utilise certain forms of spyware, could be so reckless in how it handled personal information. And it raised questions about whether similar incidents had happened in the past. Bruce McClintock, a seasoned barrister who had been appointed by the NSW Government to oversee ICAC, to act as its

watchdog, scathingly described it as a 'serious admin-
istrative failure, which has had unfair and detrimental
consequences for Ms Berejiklian'.[10]

The mistake gave valuable ammunition to critics
of the commission who maintained that it had not
only overreached in the Berejiklian case, it simply
wasn't competent enough to wield the immense
power that it held. Philip Ruddock told the ABC:
'People are not put on trial on the basis of claims, or
as I sometimes say, by innuendo. They establish first
that there is a substantial case to answer. And that
has not happened.'[11] He went on to say that part of
the problem was that Gladys Berejiklian wasn't being
investigated for corruption but for probity.

It was a fine distinction, the argument—regularly
made by Berejiklian's supporters—that while she
may have breached the rules around probity by not
revealing her relationship with Maguire, she had
not acted corruptly. And it highlighted one of the
misapprehensions concerning ICAC's work. The
breaching of ministerial standards is in fact corruption, just as probity failures are corruption. Both
Mike Baird and Gladys Berejiklian had made it so.

When NSW Labor powerbroker Eddie Obeid
became the focus of ICAC's investigative functions
in late 2012, there was widespread outrage over
how he had been able to engage in his sordid web

of corrupt dealings for so long. Among a slew of recommendations by ICAC in its staggering reports on Obeid's conduct, was the recommendation to tighten the ministerial code of conduct, specifically by making a substantial breach of that code constitute corrupt conduct.

Traditionally, the premier of the day was the person who oversaw ministerial rules at the state level, just as the prime minister held their fellow politicians to account at the federal level. But there was a flaw in this approach. If a premier or prime minister was unable or unwilling to enforce the rules that governed their ministers' behaviour, little recourse was available. There had been countless examples of ministers escaping sanction. Fundamentally, ICAC was asking to be granted the power to be the real authority on these rules. The agency itself would become a powerful deterrent when it came to ministers refusing to toe the line.

And that's exactly what Baird did. In October 2016, he strengthened the NSW ministerial code, setting out clear provisions around conflicts of interest. He also made changes to prevent ministers from pressuring public servants to change their advice. He was very proud of this at the time, declaring in a statement: 'This makes the Code for Ministers in NSW the toughest in the nation.'[12]

When Gladys Berejiklian became premier, she consolidated this initiative by signing off on her own version of the code, which required that breaches be considered corrupt conduct by ICAC. That was why Berejiklian had urged Maguire to resign from parliament when it seemed likely he had breached these rules. It was why she'd asked John Sidoti to resign from her ministry when he became the focus of an ICAC investigation. In both cases, it was about these same rules and whether they were being followed.

This may be Berejiklian's greatest failure. She expected great things from those around her, the highest standards of probity and good governance. She cultivated a belief that she stuck to and played by the rules. But even though she'd set the rules, when it came to her relationship with Maguire, she didn't think she needed to follow them.

Ruddock's argument around probity and corruption being separate and distinct matters also illustrated a cultural attitude concerning the business of government. Former ICAC assistant commissioner Anthony Whealy bristles at this oft-repeated perspective, which seeks to be dismissive of how grant funding—that is, public money—is allocated and used. 'Maguire was deliberately manipulating the finances of the state of New South Wales and using his relationship with her

[Berejiklian] to do it,' Whealy tells me. 'And on one view she was a willing participant in that.'

Whealy also sees little substance in the argument that the fate of Berejiklian echoed a pattern in which ICAC targeted and brought down state premiers. The claim is partly based on Nick Greiner resigning in mid-1992 in the wake of an ICAC investigation. And in 2014, Barry O'Farrell resigned after an appearance at ICAC, in circumstances that nobody saw coming.

ICAC was scrutinising Australian Water Holdings, in particular the credibility of one of its directors. When Nick Di Girolamo was asked a series of questions about political gifts, he revealed that he had given a bottle of wine to O'Farrell. The premier had been called as a witness, largely to test the quality of Di Girolamo's evidence, and was never under scrutiny from the commission. He was adamant that he had never received a bottle of wine from Di Girolamo—that is, until the materialisation at the commission of a handwritten note from O'Farrell thanking Di Girolamo for the bottle of wine.

Whealy didn't preside over that hearing, but he recalls being at the commission the day after O'Farrell's appearance. There was a mood of dismay. Nobody had wanted to bring down the premier, least of all the commissioner at the time, Megan Latham. 'She said, "Oh this is terrible, this could bring down the government,"' recalls Whealy. 'Because it just created a complete distraction from the real issues. But in fairness they had to let O'Farrell's lawyers know what happened.'

O'Farrell corrected his evidence and then resigned, describing the incident as a memory lapse. And when ICAC published its final report, it stressed that at no stage had O'Farrell been accused of any wrongdoing. ICAC hadn't targeted the premier. His undoing was entirely his own mistake.

Another common myth about ICAC is that its decisions to hold public hearings are made without any real contemplation of the facts, that they are effectively show trials. This overlooks the important point that ICAC's commissioners are actually required to undertake an extremely involved process before commencing a public inquiry. They need to balance the public interest in exposing allegations of corruption with the private interests of individuals.

So, does the claim that ICAC overreached in Berejiklian's case stack up? Not according to Bruce McClintock. The ICAC inspector never shied away from criticising the agency when the need arose. When he received complaints from members of the public about ICAC's decision regarding Berejiklian, he decided to carry out an investigation. He found that, based on the material the commission had gathered, its decision was entirely reasonable. McClintock also found that ICAC's call to make its announcement during the COVID outbreak was appropriate. 'Had it failed to do so,' he wrote in his report, 'it could itself have been justifiably accused of failing to perform its significant statutory functions and, indeed, of partiality towards the former Premier.'[13]

There is one other important matter that McClintock touched on. Keen observers had noticed that, curiously, ICAC's three permanent commissioners had appointed an acting commissioner—Ruth McColl—to oversee Berejiklian's hearing. McClintock clarified that this was due to a funding dispute between ICAC and the NSW Government. The commissioners were worried this disagreement could undermine the integrity of their investigations at a time when the premier herself was being investigated over potential conflicts of interest. Out of an abundance of caution, they appointed McColl to oversee the inquiry to ensure there couldn't be any perceived conflict of interest on the commission's part. McClintock found this went above and beyond what was required—it wasn't even necessary.

All of this serves as a useful illustration of how and why it is so important for powerful government entities and representatives—whether they are anti-corruption bodies or the premier of the state—to ensure that they are beyond reproach when managing conflicts of interest. Caution is always the best approach when it comes to matters of probity. ICAC's commissioners understood that. Berejiklian did not.

~

One of Berejiklian's most strident defences was that whenever she awarded taxpayer funds, she made the decision in the best interests of the community. It was an argument regularly trotted out by her supporters as well, in addition to claiming that no-one had really been harmed by what had transpired. Riverina Conservatorium of Music CEO Hamish Tait and board chair Andrew Wallace would dispute that.

Back in 2018, Tait and Wallace learnt that the lease on the conservatorium's premises in Wagga was about to expire, and the organisation would shortly be homeless. The Riverina Conservatorium of Music is a feeder school for hundreds of regional music students from across inland New South Wales. Its loss would be devastating to the local arts community. So the executives did what any community group would do in a time of need: they turned to their local MP, Daryl Maguire. Wallace recalls that Maguire was enthusiastic about supporting them. He helped them with a proposal they had prepared, which won them $10 million in government funding. They were also given a new lease at another site in Wagga where they could finally pursue a purpose-built facility.

What Tait and Wallace did not know was that, behind the scenes, Maguire had asked Berejiklian to help him secure the funding. During the ICAC hearings, Maguire was asked whether he considered the conservatorium part of his legacy. He initially fended off the question, responding that the organisation had needed a home, and he wasn't going to apologise for helping them. But when pressed, he thought for a moment and then said: 'You could say that, yes.' The reality was that, for Maguire, the conservatorium was a vanity project. In intercepted calls with Berejiklian, he repeatedly referred to it as 'my conservatorium'.

The conservatorium's CEO and chair knew nothing of this. They first learnt of the extraordinary attention they were about to face when ICAC published its media release advising that Berejiklian was now under investigation. The fallout was that, while parts of the local community were supportive, others feared the conservatorium was in league with the disgraced MP and gave it a wide berth.

'You go to the local member in good faith, expecting that this person will act for you, and take your case to the government when necessary.

That's their job. That's their role,' Tait tells me. 'When organisations, community institutions like the Riverina Conservatorium are dragged into this, it's very distressing.'

Maguire's intention may have been at least partly honourable. Perhaps he did care about the project. But ultimately, through his attempts to leverage his own relationship with the then premier, a small community organisation suffered greatly. A second stage of funding is now under scrutiny and far from guaranteed, which Tait and Wallace believe has been driven by the taint of the ICAC investigation into Maguire. They're unsure if they'll actually get the funds they need to build a new facility. 'It sort of becomes part of a political mud-slinging game, you know, one side against the other in government,' says Tait.

It's worth pointing out that neither Tait nor Wallace blame ICAC for any of this, and they both support the creation of a federal integrity agency as well. But they do feel that they have been dragged through the mud by Maguire's actions. 'It's just been a really, really damaging thing for us all at the moment,' Tait says.

Berejiklian can't escape responsibility for this. While it was Maguire who first tarnished the conservatorium through his actions, she strongly backed him in. And she approved the first stage of funding through a crucial Cabinet meeting, without ever disclosing her relationship with Maguire. She failed to exercise the great responsibility that comes with holding the public's purse strings.

~

Either you are close to the only human being covering this to see the secret truth and have a special genius and insight, or you are badly, embarrassingly, and very publicly wrong. I suspect you are mistaken thinking it is the first. I can't tell if your increasingly ridiculous coverage is willingly malicious or you just don't have a clue what actually goes on.

This was the text that Yoni Bashan, *The Australian*'s state political reporter, found waiting for him on his phone on a Saturday morning in September 2020. It was from one of Gladys Berejiklian's media advisers. The adviser was displeased by what they saw as Bashan's overly critical attacks on their office. They appeared to have been particularly incensed by an analysis piece Bashan had written suggesting that a fractious blow-up between Berejiklian and then deputy premier John Barilaro showed a failure of leadership.

The 200-word spray continued with more personal attacks: 'The more you write these clearly ill-informed articles and opinion pieces the more I hear the phrase "what on earth is wrong with that guy" (from ministers, MPs, and journos) and the more irrelevant you become.'

The premier had allies in Sydney's press gallery, but Bashan wasn't one of them. *The Australian*'s coverage of Berejiklian had been even-handed up until it emerged she was in a relationship with Maguire. Now, there were increasingly critical stories about her government in the paper. These included a number of strong news breaks from Bashan. As a consequence, he quickly found himself frozen out.

Many political reporters rely to some extent on carefully placed 'drops' from government media offices, and Bashan is certainly quick to acknowledge this symbiotic relationship. Governments want journalists onside so they can extract favourable coverage. The reporters need to find a way to keep governments talking to them, while simultaneously reporting fairly on what happens. That can be a fine line.

Bashan believes his reporting on Berejiklian was fair. He raised legitimate questions about the ICAC inquiry and the government's handling of COVID-19. And yet he was confronted by what he felt were increasingly personal and hostile attacks on him. 'There were times when I felt that it was so personal that I felt that the objective was to try and have me moved on from the round,' he tells me, 'and to attempt to convince my bosses that I was not capable of reporting on state politics because of some kind of inherent bias that I had.'

The peak of the pressure placed on him came when he received a tip-off that Berejiklian may not have self-isolated correctly after taking a COVID-19 test. He put in a question to the premier's office asking if this claim was true. He received a response attributable to 'background' telling him that it was incorrect. Bashan was suspicious. Why not simply put it on the record if it wasn't true?

'This is something that became a hallmark of the way Gladys dealt with the media,' he says. 'Her office would provide you with a quote and very often it would not be attributable to anyone. Which is kind of a very devious way of dealing with journalists. You don't have anything on the record to say it's not true, and that becomes very messy when you're trying to stand up a story about whether or not the premier did or did not self-isolate correctly. It's a denial that is not actually a denial.'

Bashan kept digging. He went back to the premier's office a second time and received another denial. But it came with what he interpreted as a threat. He was told that if he printed the COVID-test claim, he and his sources would look very silly, that he would be embarrassed and humiliated.

The story was run one afternoon on *The Australian*'s website, and other journalists quickly picked it up. The next morning, Berejiklian gave a number of television interviews. She finally conceded to Lisa Millar on *ABC News Breakfast* that she had not self-isolated. 'For me it was very typical of what Gladys endeavoured to do as a premier,' Bashan says. 'She would do the wrong thing and then she would conceal the truth.'

Berejiklian's office would later tell the ABC's *Media Watch* that it believed the specific allegations Bashan put to it were incorrect, and it was these claims it was responding to, but that the final story did not contain the inaccurate allegations.

There were other examples of this. Andrew Clennell was a regular critic of Berejiklian, notably calling her out at a press conference, and describing a culture of 'bullying and intimidation' emanating from her office. He recalls an incident that occurred in the lead-up to the NSW election in March 2019, where Berejiklian berated him at a bus stop over his unfavourable coverage.

Berejiklian's evasiveness was also a key part of her responses to the ICAC investigation. When I first asked about her role in setting aside funds for the Clay Target Association grant, she told me: 'I understand all those arrangements went through the normal processes. I don't intervene in those processes.' She made it sound as though she was a distant participant in the funding process. Except she had intervened. In fact, she had been involved in the actual decision to approve the funding, and she had also backed it in behind the scenes.

In October 2020, One Nation Senator Mark Latham got up in the NSW Parliament and, reciting from the mistakenly uploaded ICAC transcript, revealed that Daryl Maguire had a key to Gladys Berejiklian's home, a detail that was not public knowledge at the time. Opposition leader Jodi McKay followed up with a query to Berejiklian about the key in question time. The premier responded with: 'Today and in the last little while I've heard and read things which are practically factually incorrect. And I've chosen not to respond, because there is a process in place.'

But the salient fact was true. Maguire did have a key to Berejiklian's home. That at least was not 'practically factually incorrect'. So what was? Berejiklian never explained it. The only thing that was clear was that she had done everything she could to cast doubt on the claim on the floor of parliament.

'I cut Barilaro's staff's throat today,' Daryl Maguire told Gladys Berejiklian in a phone call on 13 September 2017, one that was never played in the public hearings.

'Good,' she replied.

In this ranting and raving call, Maguire laid bare his grievances with Berejiklian's second in command, her Nationals deputy John Barilaro, and with the bureaucrats he saw standing in his way. 'CSU are all over it, CSU are furious with Barilaro's office,' he said, in an apparent reference to Charles Sturt University— the specific nature of the dispute that Maguire was weighing into wasn't clear, although it appeared to relate to some funding assistance the university had sought. 'They said those people know nothing, right, so all over the place, they've got no idea. You got big, big problems.'

Moments earlier, as Maguire complained about those who might panic on getting advice from a public servant, Berejiklian said: 'But I ignore the advice. I don't worry about it.'

This was a world apart from the carefully cultivated public image that the then premier presented to the world. It was certainly far removed from her claim of being a measured and considered politician who took into account all the advice she received.

Those who regularly listened to Kyle and Jackie O's morning radio program over the years would have been familiar with Gladys Berejiklian's regular appearances on the Sydney-based show. They were light, breezy. We got a sense of the playfulness of the premier, her awkward humour. In one interview, she was only too willing to spell out the word 'suck', so great was her dislike of swearing and crude language. This was a very different side of Berejiklian to what emerged during the ICAC investigation.

Perhaps the most stunning part of the inquiry was what it revealed about what governing actually looked like in New South Wales, and what our most senior politicians thought about it. If the throat-cutting metaphor was anything to go by, it was vicious, sounding more like the political thriller *House of Cards* than most would have expected. On Berejiklian's part, she took no prisoners, brooked no fools. Good governance was simply about what served the government's political interests. This was the side of Gladys Berejiklian that wielded political power like a poleaxe.

As the 13 September 2017 phone call unfolded, we heard how Berejiklian saw her role:

MAGUIRE: So um, and who controls all those people?
BEREJIKLIAN: Which people are you talking about?

MAGUIRE: All those departments and all that stuff, who controls it all?
BEREJIKLIAN: Me.

Maguire argued with her. No, he said. The person who really controlled them all was Blair Comley.

Comley had been appointed secretary of the NSW Department of Premier and Cabinet by Mike Baird in 2014, and was highly regarded. Though clearly not by Berejiklian, who replied to Maguire: 'You know his days are numbered.'

'He's not dead,' continued Maguire, 'he's still alive and he's still walking. Stop telling me that right. He fucking controls them and this guy is from Treasury. This guy is influencing what ministers and everybody else think in your Cabinet room.' Maguire then complained that 'policy isn't gonna win you government, politics is', to which Berejiklian responded: 'I agree.'

Two months later, Comley was replaced by Tim Reardon. In public, Berejiklian said:

Blair has been outstanding at the helm of the department, and the NSW public service, since his appointment in 2014. It is widely recognised around Australia that under his leadership, the NSW public service has been transformed into a desirable and exciting employer of choice for those seeking a rewarding public service career, something of which I am immensely proud.[14]

It's jarring to read back over these words after hearing what Berejiklian really thought of Comley.

~

The Australian journalist Julia Baird, in her study into how the Australian media report on female politicians, identifies several key tropes that women in politics face.[15] Invariably, they are diminished as grandma MPs, or asked who should do the dishes, or they are drooled over. Baird says they can also be seen as peculiarities: 'a combination of metal and velvet, who were considered very surprising if successful and cast as unbending "iron lady" autocrats if decisive'.

The perception of Berejiklian as the leader of New South Wales perhaps fit most neatly into this latter category. Berejiklian was often cast as an iron figure, a surprising success with no personal life to speak of. She was also considered diminutive and self-deprecating—although that may well have been a mould that she helped cast herself, the easiest and least painful one to choose, if there was a choice at all.

The next statement from Baird illustrates the compelling challenge Berejiklian faced when her relationship with Maguire was revealed:

An assumption—often fostered by women to their own advantage—that women are cleaner, more ethical than men, and that their presence will bleach politics of grime, has been their greatest burden. Trumpeted as sincere, honest, and accessible, when they turn out to be human and flawed the pundits marvel and sneer.[16]

There was plenty of marvelling and sneering throughout the ICAC investigation. Berejiklian became the object of frenzied discussion. Some news outlets relished the thought that this matronly figure of the state actually had a sex life. There was an element of voyeurism to it, and at times a strong personal animus towards Berejiklian.

In light of what happened when Berejiklian's relationship became public, her attempts to shield her private life from any public attention make perfect sense. Why would any woman in politics, knowing the double standards at play, willingly expose themselves to them? Berejiklian could easily have foreseen the deluge of predatory and prurient interest she would suddenly face concerning her love life. There is more recent proof of that. Since she started dating the barrister Arthur Moses, a relationship that began after he acted on her behalf during her first appearance at ICAC, there's been steady tabloid intrigue concerning the couple, of a type that doesn't apply to male politicians.

There is a disconcerting obsession in Australia with the personal lives of our female politicians. One-time prime minister Julia Gillard experienced it when she was branded a liar and described as 'deliberately barren'. Former Labor MP Emma Husar found herself the victim of a vicious (and false) personal slur, an attempt to shame her that was so awful it cost her her seat in parliament. In each of these instances, there were striking double standards, and scrutiny far beyond anything that male political figures endure.

But many have pointed out that the high standards set for Berejiklian were far from undesirable. The writer and commentator Clementine Ford observed on the weekend of Berejiklian's resignation that it was odd to see some prominent feminist voices express sadness at this. Ford noted that while politics was undoubtedly hostile to women, it didn't mean that potentially corrupt conduct could be ignored:

The problem here isn't that we're too tough on women when it comes to corruption. It's that we're not tough enough on men. That men are supported to sail through these little blips and their careers won't be affected … I don't think that Gladys Berejiklian is being held to an unfair and unrealistic standard. I think that she is being held to the standard. That's what the standard should be. And the problem is that so many men aren't held to it at all.[17]

Berejiklian herself propagated throughout the ICAC hearings the idea that she was the unwitting dupe of Maguire while they were in a relationship. In 2018, when he made his first appearance at ICAC, she recounted her confusion, her lack of understanding, how unsure she felt—all because she trusted him. It was an argument that many have clearly sympathised with.

But there was also a dangerous thread in Berejiklian's argument, evident in one illuminating insight from a viewer who called into radio station 2GB one morning. When Fordham interviewed Berejiklian in October 2020 during her media blitz post the Maguire revelation, 'John' phoned in to offer his thoughts on the relationship:

JOHN: Good morning Ben and Gladys. Gladys um, my wife was reading the paper on the, on it yesterday and ah, she had a bit of a tear in her eye and I said what's wrong and she said, she looked me straight in the eye and said, 'Men.' Um, Gladys don't pull the pin, you've got our 110% support, um and Ben, you should know as well as I do, that when we start talking about work to our wives they just say get a life, you know.

FORDHAM: [Laughs]

JOHN: If it's not about the kids or shopping …

FORDHAM: Alright John …

JOHN: … if it's not about the kids or shopping …

FORDHAM: … I'll leave it there.[18]

Fordham sounded slightly mortified when John attempted to align him to his reasoning. There was a good reason for this. The suggestion was that women are only interested in two things: kids and shopping. When a man talks to a woman about work, it's so boring, so outside the realm of their interest, that of course they don't listen.

It was an awkward moment of radio, but in some respects it was the logical conclusion to the argument that Berejiklian had herself advanced: that she was not really interested in men's work, Maguire's work, and that as a consequence, she never knew anything. Her 'dud boyfriend' had taken advantage of her and used her.

Many have objected to this. The first female premier of New South Wales, and indeed of any state,

Kristina Keneally, wrote in *The Sydney Morning Herald* about why Berejiklian's position was so problematic for women in politics:

> Her defence, essentially, has been that her emotions got the better of her. This is precisely the same sexist argument that men have used in years gone by to keep women out of leadership roles in business and politics ... A female premier using sexist stereotypes about her gender risks unpicking decades of feminist progress. It does little for women's empowerment.[19]

Berejiklian's attempt to wash her hands of responsibility in her dealings with Maguire was, in Keneally's view, a deeply uncomfortable and sexist proposition. It robbed her of agency and did more harm than good for women in politics.

Of course, if the roles had been reversed, and a male premier failed to declare a relationship with a female MP for whom they made favourable decisions, it seems likely, based on the research Baird has conducted, that the framing of the story would have focused on the female MP and her conduct, rather than on the male premier's failure to disclose the relationship. And that is the other common critique of how the ICAC inquiry unfolded. Many people feel that Berejiklian was unfairly targeted when her male counterparts in state and federal governments seemingly have been able to get away with whatever they please.

The controversy surrounding Berejiklian's awarding of grant funding also invites questions over why male politicians rarely face consequences for pork-barrelling. There have been several recent high-profile cases of federal male politicians award-ing grant funding to projects that potentially give the appearance of a conflict of interest, and facing only limited scrutiny.

To take one example, when he was home affairs minister, Peter Dutton approved a one-off $880 000 grant to a retail association that had made a $1500 political donation to the Queensland Liberal National Party (LNP)—at an event Dutton attended—for the purpose of personally supporting him. The grant to the Queensland-based National Retail Association was awarded from a fund earmarked to support crime prevention efforts. It was assessed as value-for-money, but legal experts raised concerns about a potential conflict of interest due to the LNP donation. Dutton faced questioning over the matter in federal parliament, with the then minister claiming that suggestions the government had done anything other than support a worthy project were non-sense, and that 'the baseless suggestion that I have or would be influenced by a lawful donation to the LNP is false and highly defamatory'.[20] The matter soon disappeared.

The key reason for such a double standard is the structural issues in our federal system. It is the absence of a robust integrity framework in federal politics that makes it so easy for politicians to skirt around rules and codes of conduct. While there's no suggestion the grant Dutton awarded raised any integrity issues, there was no watchdog looking over the shoulder of politicians and monitoring their compliance and accountability, ready to ask the question. In the absence of a federal integrity body, there will always be examples of political figures—irrespective of their party affiliations—who evade scrutiny in a way that their state counterparts cannot.

At this point, it may also be worth reflecting on another powerful woman in New South Wales who found herself resigning from a position of influence. In 2016, ICAC's first female commissioner, Megan Latham, found herself in an extraordinary tussle with the state government. Similar to the tensions that existed during the Berejiklian inquiry, the government was placing immense pressure on the commission over how it was conducting itself.

This tension had partly arisen because of a politically contentious investigation into then Crown prosecutor Margaret Cunneen. Cunneen was heard on tape appearing to discuss how she had encouraged her daughter-in-law to delay a breath test, a claim she denied. ICAC planned to hold a private inquiry, away from the public gaze. But Cunneen took it to the Supreme Court, challenging the commission's jurisdiction in holding the inquiry. She eventually won in the High Court and was cleared of any wrongdoing. The saga left ICAC battered, and Mike Baird's government subsequently passed retrospective legislation to ensure that some findings of corrupt conduct couldn't be overturned.

Amid all of this, a furious public campaign was waged against Megan Latham. It felt personal. *The Australian* raged day after day about ICAC. Latham was papped at parties, pursued relentlessly by the media. Eventually, she resigned. In a podcast recorded in September 2020 with Jane Caro, she gave this account of her time as ICAC commissioner:

> It kind of never occurred to me that they [the government] would treat me very differently. It became clear to me they were treating me differently by the fact I didn't kind of sit there and simper and smile and appease them … It was a revelation to me that the people who were operating at that political level really didn't understand that ICAC

was a standing royal commission, and didn't really understand what that meant, and didn't really understand anything about the procedures that we went through or the processes that we adopted … The shock, I think, it was like they wanted to reduce me to another female bureaucrat who they could manage. And they were always going to find me resistant to that way of managing me.[21]

Latham's remarks are a useful explanation of the misapprehensions that many in government hold about what anti-corruption bodies do. They also serve to illustrate how she viewed the treatment she received from men in government, including the attempts to push her aside.

It is a world apart from Gladys Berejiklian's position. We see in Berejiklian's argument the view that she was a woman with no agency. The suggestion was that the most powerful, savvy, impressive political operator in New South Wales blindly trusted her boyfriend and never really listened to him when he spoke. Latham, on the other hand, was *all* about agency.

~

Berejiklian's one big lie was her relationship with Maguire. It was something she kept from everyone.

And that big lie spawned dozens of smaller ones. Berejiklian's attempts to hold on to power, to downplay the status of her involvement with the Wagga MP, were a key part of her own defence.

During the public ICAC hearing, Berejiklian revealed that she had told just two people about her relationship with Maguire, after his involvement in the corruption probe emerged in 2018. The first was a friend who encouraged her to go to her chief of staff. Sarah Cruickshank needed to know, said the friend. Berejiklian did just that. But when Cruickshank gave her evidence, she was adamant that Berejiklian told her it was a historic relationship. Berejiklian disputed this during the hearing, but ICAC ultimately found that she had lied to her friend. She was, in the commission's dry words, 'not a satisfactory witness'. This was one of the many smaller lies that followed Berejiklian, untruths that increasingly damaged her credibility and integrity, even among those closest to her.

After Berejiklian's November 2021 appearance at ICAC, the action moved behind the scenes. ICAC's counsel assisting, Scott Robertson, would have made submissions about what findings they believed Ruth McColl should make. It was during this period that ICAC quietly published dozens more documents from the inquiry. They included the brief transcript of an intercepted phone call between Berejiklian and Maguire from 11 March 2018:

BEREJIKLIAN: Why, what have you got planned?

MAGUIRE: Oh I don't have anything planned but I thought I might like to go and meet your parents now that I've got all this out of the way.

BEREJIKLIAN: Oh, okay.

MAGUIRE: Mmm, so I …

BEREJIKLIAN: That's nice.

MAGUIRE: Yeah I thought I'll go and say hello to them or I thought you can do two things. You can either bring them to the farm for a couple of days …

BEREJIKLIAN: Mmm.

MAGUIRE: … and say hello. Or um, we can tee up a day and we'll have a dinner with them and just say this is who I am.

BEREJIKLIAN: Okay, okay.

Berejiklian had acknowledged having a discussion with Maguire about introducing him to her parents. But that meeting never happened. As for the call, no explanation was given about what happened after it took place. And so, when reading the transcript now, it seems strikingly at odds with other parts of Berejiklian's evidence.

In her 2021 appearance at ICAC, Berejiklian said that disclosing the relationship with Maguire was never something that crossed her mind. 'The threshold for me was would I introduce him to my parents, would I introduce him to my sisters, was I confident it was going to be something to last a distance of time, and I didn't feel that,' she told the acting commissioner.

This was Berejiklian's great secret. She did everything she could to publicly distance herself from Maguire, and it eventually unravelled her career and her life.

~

On 29 June 2023, two ICAC officials identified only as Catherine and Louis walked into a room in the NSW Parliament, sat down on red horsehair chairs, and placed two enormous volumes on a table. A gaggle of cameras was there to capture the moment that the anti-corruption body's findings against Daryl Maguire and Gladys Berejiklian were pushed across the table and into the hands of Legislative Assembly Speaker Greg Piper.

It had been more than twenty months since Berejiklian had appeared at ICAC, and much had changed. A federal Labor government had swept to power in May 2022, in part on a platform of integrity—two days after the ICAC report was published, the newly formed National Anti-Corruption Commission became operational. Then, in March 2023, the government headed by Berejiklian's successor, Dominic Perrottet, lost power to Labor, having limped through a series of scandals. Now, after a long wait, the public was about to be confronted by a devastating assessment of a former NSW premier's character and legacy.

ICAC's findings, the most serious ever levelled against a political leader in New South Wales, make brutal reading. ICAC found Berejiklian engaged in serious corrupt conduct regarding the awarding of the shooting association and conservatorium grants in Maguire's electorate. It concluded Berejiklian breached public trust by shoring up these grants, which she knew Maguire sought, and by failing to disclose the conflict of interest. It also found that Berejiklian's relationship with Maguire clearly warranted disclosure. Her failure to reveal it was not an 'honest error of judgment'. Rather, she 'deliberately failed' to disclose it, despite having the opportunity to do so at key meetings concerning the grants. ICAC also found the claim that Berejiklian treated Maguire like any other MP to be 'fallacious', and that she'd breached the very ministerial code she'd expected her colleagues to follow.

Remarkably, the report reveals that Berejiklian argued she was above the law. Her legal team attempted to mount the case that the ministerial code of conduct—the document all ministers swear to uphold, and which Berejiklian herself signed off on— didn't apply to her at all. ICAC roundly rejected this.

A second key finding is perhaps the gravest: that Berejiklian reasonably suspected Maguire was corrupt, and failed to do anything about it. ICAC found her claim that she suspected nothing wasn't credible, asserting Berejiklian made a 'wilful attempt … to keep herself blind' to Maguire's conduct. She had 'clearly connected the dots' between the land deals Maguire talked about and his attempts to profit from them. She knew that having precise knowledge of Maguire's commission 'could raise difficulties if shared with her'. And when he confided to her in 2018 that he had been summoned to appear before ICAC at a separate inquiry, there was simply no way Berejiklian could not have known something was very wrong.

The 700-page report is packed with assessments that chip away at the former premier's once pristine veneer of integrity. ICAC found that, as a witness, she 'downplayed' the significance of her conversations with Maguire. In addition, her account of conversations with her former chief of staff

Sarah Cruickshank 'smacks of reconstruction and wishful thinking'. Time after time, the commission rejects her explanations.

Perhaps the ultimate humiliation for a former premier who carefully cultivated her image through various news outlets was *The Sydney Morning Herald*'s response the day after ICAC's findings were released. The newspaper printed a picture of Berejiklian in parliament, headlined by the words: 'A CORRUPT LIAR: ICAC'.

However, while Maguire himself will face a referral to the NSW Director of Public Prosecutions and possible prosecution, Berejiklian will not, ICAC having decided against this. The commission found that Berejiklian's conduct, while it was corrupt, did not meet the higher bar of a criminal offence.

The ICAC findings matter. The commission's report also sets out important recommendations for strengthening how public funds are awarded, and plugging the gaps that allowed Maguire to engage in his various deals. But the extreme delay in finalising the report gave ICAC's critics—and Berejiklian's allies—valuable ammunition. Within an hour of the report being made public, Liberal MP Matt Kean tweeted: 'So it has taken ICAC two years to tell us that Gladys Berejiklian has not engaged in criminal conduct.' Federal Opposition leader Peter Dutton said Berejiklian simply 'chose a bum', that she wasn't corrupt and should 'hold her head high'.

Even supporters of the commission believed something had gone awry. Geoffrey Watson SC and former Supreme Court judge Anthony Whealy said the delay had undermined the institution's credibility. ICAC now faces a review by its own watchdog.

~

Corruption and graft flourish when people say nothing. Daryl Maguire was able to get his way for so long because he took advantage of this silence. Gladys Berejiklian had numerous opportunities to stand up and say she thought something was wrong, but she said nothing. ICAC found there was overwhelming evidence that Berejiklian failed to root out corruption when she suspected it was occurring. When you set aside the painful details of a relationship gone wrong, it boils down to this: a state leader turned a blind eye to a colleague's corrupt conduct.

Silence has a strange way of creeping into public conversation. In the wake of ICAC's findings, perhaps the most striking silence came from new Labor Premier Chris Minns, who refused to even describe Berejiklian's conduct as corrupt. A generous, albeit cynical, view is that he knows how popular Berejiklian remains and fears isolating prospective voters. A less generous view is that he fears corruption lurks within his own ranks, and he doesn't wish to give his political enemies any ammunition. Regardless, Minns' refusal to condemn corruption shows how fragile our political system has become.

The institutions working to weed out corruption face ferocious criticism from certain politicians and their allies. For the first time, we have a national integrity agency keeping an eye on federal politics, but it faces an enormous task in changing entrenched practices. It is bound to discover corruption in the political class, and in doing so, it will make enemies— much like its NSW counterpart. Whether or not it will be hampered or neutralised by these enemies remains to be seen.

~

Gladys Berejiklian remains on the minds of many Australians. Those who believe she was wronged, and the many women in the country who see her as a role model because of her rise to power, hold out strong hopes she will again emerge in public life. Some of her colleagues in the Liberal Party also hope for this. Meanwhile, photographers follow her around. She's papped in bookstores with her boyfriend, at restaurants with girlfriends, outside her home. It has gone national, too. These stories keep coming because news editors know their audiences remain keen to read about her. We still can't get enough of Gladys.

Berejiklian is currently back on the corporate ladder with Optus. It's strange to see the former premier being wheeled out by the telco to front the media, knowing that ICAC deliberated about her for so many months. Optus too doesn't seem to have any concerns that a former premier who was found to have engaged in serious corrupt conduct occupies an executive position with them.

The speculation about Berejiklian's future continues: will she return to politics, perhaps elevated to the federal level as the Liberal Party struggles to rebuild itself? Her friends and colleagues point to a deep hunger she has to rehabilitate her image. Resigning from leadership of the state while embroiled in a corruption inquiry was never how she saw the end of her time in politics. She apparently feels she has much more to give. Perhaps when the next federal election comes around in 2025, she will make her move.

Gladys Berejiklian has been branded with one of the most serious findings a premier has ever faced, but she has never been the type to slink away into the night. Everything she's done to this point reveals few limits to her ambition. If anyone can do it, it's her.

But how she will be received on the national stage, in a new parliament inundated by a surge of women who have campaigned on integrity, is far from certain. As a lone voice among a group of middling men, she stood out. Whether she could continue to do so, and how she might fare testing the appetite of the electorate for a political figure who turned a blind eye to corruption, is far from certain.

What is beyond doubt is that this will not be the last we see of Gladys Berejiklian.

ACKNOWLEDGEMENTS

I owe thanks to the Australian Broadcasting Corporation for the great privilege of being able to do public interest journalism. In particular, thanks to Justin Stevens, Leigh Sales, Marian Wilkinson, Suzanne Dredge, Alex McDonald and John Lyons for their guidance and for always backing the tough stories. Thanks also to Louise Adler, Paul Smitz and Greg Bain for their guidance in shaping this book.

NOTES

1 ABC News, 'NSW Premier Says She Won't Resign after Explosive ICAC Revelations', 12 October 2020, https://www.youtube.com/watch?v=CJfkj9hFU3s (viewed November 2022).

2 *The Sydney Morning Herald*, 'Berejiklian's Halo Has Not Slipped, Survey Shows', 25 November 2021, https://www.smh.com.au/politics/nsw/berejiklian-s-halo-has-not-slipped-survey-shows-20211124-p59bop.html (viewed November 2022).

3 Hansard, 'Daryl Maguire Inaugural Speech', 1999, https://www.parliament.nsw.gov.au/Hansard/Pages/HansardResult.aspx#/docid/HANSARD-1323879322-19849/link/12 (viewed November 2022).

4 Michael Photios, 'How an Armenian Migrant Girl Slayed the Labor Dragon', *The Australian*, 24 March 2019, https://www.theaustralian.com.au/nation/politics/how-an-armenian-migrant-girl-slayed-the-labor-dragon/news-story/b5e592ee47eedc0bc860eaf73094693d (viewed November 2022).

5 Anne Davies, 'Berejiklian Concedes $140m Grant Scheme Was Pork-Barrelling, But Says "It's Not Unique to Our Government"', *The Guardian*, 26 November 2020, https://www.theguardian.com/australia-news/2020/nov/26/berejiklian-admits-140m-grant-scheme-was-pork-barrelling-as-approval-documents-revealed (viewed November 2022).

6 Sean Rubinsztein-Dunlop and Echo Hui, 'When the Fixer from Wagga Met the Conmen from Shanghai', ABC Investigations, 28 July 2021, https://www.abc.net.au/news/2021-07-28/how-nsw-mp-daryl-maguire-helped-jimmy-liu-s-companies/100297392 (viewed November 2022).

7 Paul Farrell and Alex McDonald, 'Gladys Berejiklian Oversaw Fund that Set Aside $5.5m for Project Backed By Daryl Maguire', ABC News, 3 December 2020, https://www.abc.net.au/news/2020-12-03/gladys-berejiklian-daryl-maguire-clay-target-association/12937658 (viewed November 2022).

8 Michael McGowan and Anne Davies, 'NSW Premier Gladys Berejiklian Resigns after ICAC Announces Investigation', *The Guardian*, 1 October 2021, https://www.theguardian.com/australia-news/2021/oct/01/nsw-premier-gladys-berejiklian-resigns-after-icac-announces-investigation (viewed November 2022).

9 Hansard, 'Commonwealth Integrity Commission', 25 November 2021, https://parlinfo.aph.gov.au/parlInfo/search/display/display.w3p;db=CHAMBER;id=chamber%2Fhansardr%2F25173%2F0128;query=Id%3A%22chamber%2Fhansardr%2F25173%2F0005%22 (viewed November 2022).

10 Office of the Inspector of the Independent Commission Against Corruption, *Report Concerning Circumstances Surrounding the Independent Commission Against Corruption's Use of Certain Telephone Intercept Material During Operation Keppel*, special report 2021/03, https://www.oiicac.nsw.gov.au/assets/oiicac/reports/special-reports/Report-concerning-circumstances-surrounding-the-Independent-Commission-Against-Corruptions-use-of-certain-telephone-intercept-material-during-Operation-Keppel-2021-03.pdf (viewed November 2022).

11 *RN Breakfast*, 'Senior NSW Liberals Critical of the Timing of ICAC's Investigation into Gladys Berejiklian', ABC Radio National, 4 October 2021, https://www.abc.net.au/radionational/programs/breakfast/nsw-liberals-icac-gladys-berejiklian/13568976 (viewed November 2022).

12 NSW Government, 'Government Toughens Ministerial Code', media release, 4 October 2016, https://www.nsw.gov.au/media-releases/government-toughens-ministerial-code (viewed November 2022).

13 Office of the Inspector of the Independent Commission Against Corruption, *Special Report By the Inspector of the Independent Commission Against Corruption Pursuant to Section 77A of the* Independent Commission Against Corruption Act 1988

Regarding the Decision to Hold a Further Public Inquiry in Operation Keppel, special report 2022/01, https://www.oiicac.nsw.gov.au/assets/oiicac/reports/special-reports/Special-Report-s-77A-ICAC-Act-regarding-the-Decision-to-Hold-a-Further-Public-Inquiry-in-Operation-Keppel-2022-01.pdf (viewed November 2022).

14 NSW Government, 'Appointment of New Secretary to DPC', media release, 10 November 2017, https://www.nsw.gov.au/media-releases/appointment-of-new-secretary-to-dpc (viewed November 2022).

15 Julia Baird, *Media Tarts*, rev. edn, ABC Books, Sydney, 2021.

16 Ibid.

17 Clementine Ford, 'This Was a Very Requested Topic …', Facebook, https://www.facebook.com/watch/?v=847754789219804&paipv=0&eav=AfYARRBesibJY1e_XcStvp97YYp4NcvpO5-jFiygjW12qLkmTYioXfRGbkqngFhRLr0 (viewed November 2022).

18 *Ben Fordham Live*, 'NSW Premier Gladys Berejiklian Bares All in Candid Interview with Ben Fordham', 2GB, 19 October 2020, https://www.2gb.com/nsw-premier-gladys-berejiklian-bares-all-in-candid-interview-with-ben-fordham/ (viewed November 2022).

19 Kristina Keneally, 'I Backed Berejiklian's Right to Power, But Her Fall Is Not a Blow for Feminism', *The Sydney Morning Herald*, 7 October 2021, https://www.smh.com.au/national/i-backed-berejiklian-s-right-to-power-but-her-fall-is-not-a-blow-for-feminism-20211006-p58xkw.html (viewed November 2022).

20 Paul Farrell and Alex McDonald, 'Peter Dutton's Office Fast-Tracked One-Off Grant Proposal Days after Donation Given to Support Him', ABC News, 10 February 2021, https://www.abc.net.au/news/2021-02-10/peter-dutton-office-fast-tracked-grant-proposal-after-donation/13126496 (viewed November 2022).

21 *Women with Clout*, 'Megan Latham', Podchaser, 8 September 2020, https://www.podchaser.com/podcasts/women-with-clout-719735/episodes/megan-latham-74024143 (viewed November 2022).

IN THE NATIONAL INTEREST

Other books on the issues that matter: